Original title:
The Paradise of the Seas

Copyright © 2025 Creative Arts Management OÜ
All rights reserved.

Author: Tobias Sterling
ISBN HARDBACK: 978-1-80581-697-3
ISBN PAPERBACK: 978-1-80581-224-1
ISBN EBOOK: 978-1-80581-697-3

Gardens of the Sea's Embrace

In the depths of blue, fish wear a hat,
A crab plays guitar, how about that?
Starfish throwing parties on coral reefs,
While seahorses dance, who needs beliefs?

Jellyfish bouncing like balloons in air,
Octopuses juggling without a care,
With bubbles that sparkle and giggles galore,
The undersea laughs, who could ask for more?

Turtles in shades, they paddle with style,
Whales singing tunes that stretch for a mile,
Dolphins surf waves, they're quite the sight,
Making ocean waves until the night.

As the sun sets low on the wavy crest,
Mermaids toast shells, it's all for the best,
With laughter and splashes, they sway through the tide,
In this watery realm, fun won't subside!

The Tide's Embrace

The waves dance with a goofy grace,
A splash of water, a seaweed chase.
Jellyfish jiggle, like clumsy friends,
While sea turtles giggle as daylight ends.

Drifting on surfboards, the seagulls dive,
Chasing the tides, they feel alive.
Mermaids with laughter, snorkels on heads,
They play hide and seek, in underwater beds.

Castles of Sand and Seafoam

In the sand, we build tall towers,
With moats of foam and salty showers.
A crab with a crown rules over the scene,
Declaring the day a crustacean's dream.

Buckets and shovels, a whimsical gang,
As seagulls squawk out their beachy twang.
A sandcastle throne, the scrappy king's flair,
With jellybean jewels, for all to share.

Fables of the Driftwood

A stick's tale unwinds on the shore,
It floated from lands we can't explore.
With stories of pirates, and mermaid jams,
It dreams of adventures with clams and hams.

Each piece of driftwood is wise and old,
Whispering secrets in the stories told.
They giggle and creak as the waves pass by,
Waving their branches to fish flying high.

Candles Adrift on the Water

Tiny lights bob in the evening stream,
With hopes and wishes, they dance and beam.
Floating like dreams, all aglow,
They chase the moon's laughter, row by row.

But one little candle gets lost in the fun,
Floating in circles, chasing the sun.
It hops on a wave, gives a cheeky grin,
Saying, "I'm off—let the night begin!"

Embracing the Nautical Dawn

The sun peeks over waves so spry,
Squawking gulls sing like they can fly.
Fish in a frenzy, what a sight!
Flip-flops lost in a splashy fight.

Sailboats wobble in a game of chase,
Captains giggle, all smiles on their face.
A jellyfish winks, a curious dance,
As the waves beckon for another chance.

The Shores of Forgotten Whispers

Upon the sand, I found a shoe,
Worn by a pirate or a squeaky zoo?
With seashells giggling, they tell their tales,
Of sunburned noses and ocean gales.

A crab in a tuxedo, quite the sight,
Dancing to tunes of the moonlit night.
Seagulls wearing hats, how absurd,
Join the fun with a flapping word.

Rhapsody of the Dancing Waves

The waves are dancing with a silly grace,
Splashing beachgoers in a watery race.
Paddles thrash, and laughter soars,
As mermaids giggle behind ocean doors.

A dog on a surfboard, what a blast,
Stealing boat snacks, having a laugh.
The tide rolls in with a playful shove,
Sending sandcastles flying, oh what love!

Harmonies of the Endless Horizon

Under the sun, a hammock swings,
As seagulls complain about humans' flings.
A beach ball bounces, setting the scene,
While sandals lie abandoned, so pristine.

Snorkelers bubbling, lost in their quest,
Finding more fish than they might have guessed.
The horizon laughs, as waves give chase,
In this silly dance, we've found our place.

Colors of Reflection

Waves tickle shores, in a playful spree,
Bright hues splash, like a painting at sea.
Fish wear their outfits, quite flashy and neat,
While crabs do the cha-cha, with rhythm and beat.

Seagulls don sunglasses, they strut with glee,
Sunbathers building castles, like it's a decree.
Flip-flops are flying, oh what a sight,
As beach balls go bouncing, into the night.

Luminous Depths Awaiting

In waters below, where jellyfish glow,
Mermaids play poker, with octopi in tow.
Turtles navigate, all cool and sly,
While fish gossip madly, just passing by.

Coral reefs giggle at the clownfish parade,
With shrimps serving drinks, in the oceanic jade.
Dolphins read fortunes, swim by for a snack,
As bubbles of laughter unfold in a stack.

The Sea's Silent Promise

Whispers of waves, in a comical scheme,
Sharks throw a party, it's the ultimate dream.
Starfish flip-flop, in their own little way,
As pearls hold secrets, gleaming all day.

Crabs hold the mic, and sing out their fun,
With clams keeping rhythm, they're second to none.
Sea cucumbers waltz, with grace and with flair,
In a dance of delight, that's beyond compare.

Whispers of Salt and Sunlight

Under the sun, a joyful retreat,
With tide pools of treasures, an explorer's treat.
Seashells engage in clattering chat,
While mermaids giggle, "Did you see that?"

Surfboards ride waves, in an epic show,
As children chase crabs; oh what a glow!
Coconuts chuckle, with jokes they exchange,
In this sunny haven, where nothing seems strange.

A Canvas of Aquatic Wonders

Bubbles rise like tiny balloons,
Fish wear hats and sing silly tunes.
Seashells play a game of chess,
While crabs strut in their best dress.

Octopuses take selfies with flair,
Starfish dance without a care.
Jellyfish float like disco balls,
Throwing parties in underwater halls.

Celestial Currents and Dreams

Whales wear sneakers as they glide,
Turtles race with a joyful stride.
Sandy beaches host a grand parade,
With seashell trumpets and hand-made shade.

Dolphins laugh like best friends do,
Puffers puff up just for a view.
The tides brush the shore with bright confetti,
As fish throw their fins, all cool and sweaty.

The Dance of the Coral Ballet

Corals wiggle in tutus bright,
Clownfish make jokes that feel just right.
The floor is a stage where sea critters prance,
They twirl and swirl in a bubbly dance.

Sea anemones wave their arms with glee,
While shrimp are the stars of this grand marquee.
A conch shells out applause with a blare,
As every creature joins in without a care.

Reflections on an Ocean's Heart

A mirror shows fish in a deep blue trance,
Turtles chuckle at their clumsy stance.
Seagulls dive for the best food around,
And all of the waves giggle with sound.

Seashells gossip about the moon's glow,
While playful dolphins put on a show.
Every splash is a laugh, a silly surprise,
As the ocean grins with sparkling eyes.

Shores of Forgotten Tales

On shores where seagulls play,
Old pirates lose their way.
They trip on their treasure maps,
And fall in sunken traps.

The crab holds court with glee,
Disputes over who is free.
He snaps at sailors' toes,
As the ocean swells and blows.

Seashells whisper stories past,
Of fish who swim so fast.
But tales of mermaids' hair,
Are just seaweed's tangled flair.

With flip-flops and a grin,
Life's a splash, let's dive in!
A dolphin waves hello,
As the waves begin to glow.

The Heartbeat of the Ocean

The waves are like a drum,
A rhythm that's quite fun.
Each splash is a new beat,
As crabs dance on their feet.

A fish in shades of pink,
Winks while he takes a drink.
The seaweed starts to sway,
With all that ocean play.

Turtles race for the sun,
While jellyfish just shun.
They float like lazy kings,
In waters where joy sings.

Octopuses in disguise,
Play hide and seek with sighs.
Each bubble tells a joke,
Underneath the sea's cloak.

Ripples of Serenity

In calm waters, all are flaws,
As fish slip in, without a pause.
The sun sneezes, with a gleam,
Creating waves like a playful dream.

Seashells giggle on the shore,
As if they know of tales galore.
A crab conducts the seafarers,
While seagulls roll their aerial errors.

Mermaids sip their fancy tea,
With laughter that sets time free.
The peace is cracked with glee,
As dolphins play hide-and-seek.

Splash and whirl in gentle hues,
Where laughter mingles with the blues.
The ocean's heart beats loud,
As a lobster bows, feeling proud.

A Symphony of the Tides

The tides hum a goofy tune,
Beneath the lazy moon.
A clownfish wears a hat,
While the starfish points and chats.

The waves conduct a soft choir,
As sea monsters retire.
They strum on coral reefs,
With rhythms that bring reliefs.

Bubbles pop like tiny stars,
While crabs drive little cars.
The ocean floor's a stage,
Filled with laughter, all the rage.

Fish dance in watery waltz,
While seashells play the false.
Together they create delight,
In a world that's a sheer sight.

Currents of Enchantment

In a boat made of jelly, we sail on a dream,
Fish wear tiny hats, oh, what a team!
The waves giggle softly, the sun runs away,
While seagulls pull pranks, making dolphins sway.

Mermaids serve tacos, with salsa and cheer,
And crabs do the cha-cha, oh, don't be a sneer!
Underwater picnics, with sweets that won't drown,
We laugh until sunset, the best time in town.

Whims of the Wind and Waves

A whale does a cannonball, splashing so high,
While the turtles play cards, oh me, oh my!
The breeze sings a tune of a wobbly jig,
As octopuses dance, doing flips and a dig.

Clouds wear their pajamas, all soft and so light,
While squids serve us cider, spiked just right!
The horizon's a canvas, with colors so bright,
As we sail through this laughter, under the moonlight.

A Dance of Aquatic Echoes

The starfish are waltzing on a floor made of sand,
With turtles in tuxedos, looking quite grand!
Crabs pinch the rhythm with claws over rocks,
While fishes in bow ties check their funny clocks.

The bubbles bubble up, singing songs of delight,
As clownfish juggle pearls, oh, what a sight!
We twirl with the whirlpools, embrace every twirl,
In this sea of giggles, we'll dance and we'll whirl.

Nautical Starfinders

With compasses made of candy, we plot our course,
Sailing on licorice waves, full of sweet force!
The stars try to sparkle, but end up just glee,
As the moon spins a yarn about a bee on a spree.

Octopi navigate with a flair, oh so neat,
While shrimp plan the party, it'll be quite the feat!
In this world of ocean, so silly and grand,
We'll find our way home with a lollipop hand.

Guardian Spirits of the Deep.

Bubbles rise like disco lights,
Fish wear shades in neon sights.
Crabs do the cha-cha on the sand,
Octopuses play in a funky band.

Sharks are juggling starlit beams,
Mermaids prance in bubble dreams.
Seahorses giggle, tails entwined,
The deep is where the fun's designed.

Eels do twirls with graceful flair,
And turtles race without a care.
In this realm of jolly cheer,
The ocean's spirits all draw near.

Whispers of Oceanic Dreams

Whales sing tunes in jazzy ways,
Dolphins dance through foam-filled sprays.
Starfish gossip, oh what glee,
In coral castles, wild and free.

Tangled kelp becomes a swing,
As playful otters laugh and cling.
Crabs vie for the limelight's glow,
Pretending they're the stars of the show.

A clam gets shy, hides in the sand,
While seagulls cheer, a raucous band.
With every splash, joy's summoning,
In ocean realms, let laughter ring.

Beneath the Azure Canopy

Beneath the waves, where giggles play,
Jellyfish float, doing ballet.
Clownfish joke in colors bright,
Spreading joy in pure delight.

Sea turtles chat about the trend,
Of sunken treasures 'round each bend.
Anemones blush, feeling bold,
Their tentacles dance, a sight to behold.

With every splash, a tale's set free,
Of ocean antics, wild and spree.
In this world where the funny flows,
Even the seaweed strikes a pose!

Serene Tides of Tranquility

The gentle tides rock boats in glee,
While seahorses sip their herb tea.
Walruses crack jokes on the shore,
Their laughter echoes, who could want more?

In every wave, a chuckle hides,
As playful seals glide with pride.
Shells whisper secrets, share a grin,
The peaceful surf, a merry din.

Fish in tuxedos stroll the line,
While crabs complain about the brine.
With every crest, a soft reprise,
In this serene, funny paradise.

Emissaries of the Abyss

In the depths where fish wear hats,
And jellybeans float like chatty spats,
Eels dance with style, they've got some flair,
While sea cucumbers trip without a care.

Octopuses play cards on a seaweed throne,
With pirate gold, they've made it their own.
A crab in a tux gives a wink and a nod,
As sea, its vibe, gets marvelously odd.

The dolphin's got jokes that make the waves laugh,
While anchovies sunbathe on a surfboard's path.
Seahorses sip cocktails with tiny pink straws,
In an underwater bar with no laws!

Who knew the deep was such a grand show?
With bubbles of laughter, the currents all flow.
So dive in, my friend, let the fun not cease,
In this oceanic realm, we've found our peace.

Breezes of Forgotten Shores

On sandy banks where crabs discuss,
And sandcastles sway without much fuss,
Seashells gossip about the tides,
While seagulls race with sassy slides.

The mermaids giggle with shimmering hair,
Casting nets for laughter, who wouldn't dare?
They drink from coconuts, oh what a treat,
And dance on the sand with their playful feet.

Wind whispers secrets of old boat dreams,
While starfish plot under moonlight beams.
Seashells, their currency, they hold so dear,
As waves come laughing, we all cheer.

Wave goodbye to worries on this shore,
Where giggles and splashes open the door.
A paradise where funny finds a home,
Let's play in the sand, let's dance, let's roam!

A Tapestry of Aquatic Light

Bubbles rise up like giggles in air,
While corals bend colors without a care.
Fish wear bowties, the bubbles do sway,
Singing odd songs in a comical way.

Lights shimmer down from the surface above,
As clams are busy falling in love.
Anemones wave like they're in a cheer,
As sea stars tell jokes that you just need to hear.

Clownfish showing off in striped attire,
While sea turtles mime in a tangled choir.
With flippers flicking and eyes all a-twinkle,
The ocean's alive with a laugh and a sprinkle.

This underwater scene, a silly delight,
Makes every fish feel that everything's right.
So join in the fun, let your spirit ignite,
In this bubbling world of aquatic light!

Sentinels of the Deep

Guarding the depths with an eye so wide,
The fish tell tales with a giggly pride.
Seahorses stand tall in their tiny parade,
While barnacles serve snacks that're perfectly made.

Squids play tag with a splashy flair,
While crustaceans plot their next fun affair.
The sunbeams shimmer like laugh-coated rays,
As the deep sea critters start their wild phase.

With every wave comes a chuckle and cheer,
As dolphins tell stories, everyone's near.
The narwhals just grin with their long, spry horns,
Inviting all shapes from the ocean's adorns.

In this kingdom of laughter where all critters meet,
The essence of fun twines through the deep heat.
So let's dive into joy, with bubbles and gleam,
For the ocean's a realm where we all share a dream.

Treasures of the Abyssal Heart

Down in the deep, where the seaweed sways,
Fish throw a party, in their own fishy ways.
A crab with a hat, dancing on the floor,
Claims he found gold, but it's just a door!

Octopuses juggle, with balls made of glass,
While seahorses race, quite a comical class.
And clams sing a tune, off-key and absurd,
The laughter of dolphins is truly unheard!

A treasure chest opens, filled with lost socks,
And a pair of flip-flops from careless old docs.
The pearls shine brightly, but wait, what's that?
A message in a bottle? Nope, just a spat!

So let's take a dip, in this watery bash,
Where seabed treasures make quite the splash.
With laughter and bubbles, we shall not miss,
In the heart of the abyss, there's fun and bliss!

The Lure of Eternity's Waters

Waves whisper secrets, like old silly jokes,
Mermaids just giggle, they're playful old folks.
A merman, he trips on his tail quite a lot,
And tumbles through foam, in his glittery spot.

The sea turtles race on their shells made of cheese,
While gulls joke and tease with the swaying breeze.
An octopus plays cards, counting with glee,
But loses his hand to a crab, oh dear me!

The lanternfish glow, they flicker and flash,
As walruses dance in a jolly old smash.
With sea cucumbers rolling in laughter's embrace,
In waters so timeless, there's joy all over the place!

So come take a trip, where the fun never fades,
In the waves' endless laughter, and shining cascades.
With friends from the depths, we'll share a deep smile,
In the lure of these waters, we'll revel in style!

Lullaby of the Lost Isles

In the hush of the night, the islands do sing,
With coconuts dancing, what joy do they bring!
A parrot's got jokes, and the palm trees sway,
While crabs wear pajamas, it's quite the display.

The stars twinkle softly, like shells on the shore,
A starfish plays guitar, it's never a bore.
A whale hums a tune, both funny and sweet,
While the waves clap along, with their foamy feet.

The coconut drinks spill, as the lizards do cheer,
While a tortoise sings low, "I'm the king of this sphere!"
And a breeze whispers tales of the quirky and bold,
In the lull of the night, such laughter unfolds.

So here in this haven, where whimsy runs wild,
The lullaby dances, with nature's own child.
With every sweet note, let's twirl and swirl,
In the heart of the isles, join the joyful whirl!

Dance of the Ocean's Dream

In a swirl of blue, where the currents all sway,
The fish don their bows, for a grand cabaret!
Clownfish in tuxedos, they shimmy and zoom,
While jellyfish float like they own the whole room.

The turtles keep time, with a slow dancing flip,
A sea sponge spins wildly, on a bustling trip.
The starfish take turns leading the conga,
While lobsters in boots shout, "You can't go wrong here!"

In the night's liquid glow, with a shimmer and twirl,
The seaweed waves gently, in this underwater whirl.
With laughter and music, the ocean's a dream,
As fish join the dance, in a glowing moonbeam!

So gather your friends, and let's take the dive,
Where the dance of the ocean keeps all dreams alive.
With a splash and a giggle, let's sway to the sound,
In the depths of the sea, where joy knows no bound!

The Unseen Kingdom Beneath

Beneath the waves, a circus thrives,
With fish in tuxes and jellyfish jives,
Crabs doing the cha-cha, very spry,
While clams roll their eyes, oh my!

Seaweed dancers twirl and weave,
Nemo's lost, but he won't leave,
A dolphin laughs with bubbles aglow,
As octopuses put on a show.

Starfish play cards on the ocean floor,
And blowfish knock, then start to snore,
A parrotfish yells, 'This is divine!'
As clownfish joke and sip on brine.

But watch out now, the tide takes flight!
They scramble for cover, what a sight!
With each wave crash, they dance away,
In this underwater cabaret.

Flickers of Hope in the Blue

The ocean sparkles with a wink,
As fishy friends toast in a drink,
A whale sings opera, deep and grand,
While sea cucumbers lend a hand.

Bubbles are laughter, round and bright,
Turtles race at quite a fright,
The seagulls squawk, 'What's on the menu?'
As the sea stars reveal secrets too!

Coral reefs dressed for a ball,
With seaweed hats and a grand old hall,
Anemones laugh, "Oh, such a tease!"
While the clownfish giggle with great ease.

In the depths, where the light is rare,
You'll see a fish with an outrageous hair,
They flip and flop, what a funny crew,
In their watery world, so bright and blue.

Resonances of Seashell Songs

Seashells gather, their tunes combine,
Whispering secrets of the brine,
A conch blasts jokes that make us grin,
While scallops giggle, where to begin?

"Why did the fish blush?" they ask,
"Because it saw the ocean's flask!"
These funny tales from below the tide,
Bring laughter forth, where fish abide.

Clams tell stories in a hushed tone,
Of pirates lost and treasures blown,
A hermit crab who lost his shell,
Wanders off with tales to tell.

As waves sway to the rhythmic chime,
The ocean's heart beats, oh so prime,
In this underwater realm we find,
Seashells singing, all unconfined.

The Beat of Ocean's Heart

The ocean thumps like a giant's drum,
With fish conga lines, oh so fun!
Starfish flail, trying to keep pace,
While seahorses waltz with elegance and grace.

The waves clap loud, a bouncy cheer,
While playful otters chug their beer,
A pufferfish adds a little flair,
Just don't ask him to share his air!

Coral has rhythm, it sways and dips,
As dolphins jump, performing flips,
The tinkling shells join in the throng,
Echoing laughter in a jubilant song.

In this ocean festivity, time takes a break,
The sea creatures gather for fun's sweet sake,
With a splash, a laugh, a flip, and a smart quirk,
The heartbeat of water, now turns to work.

Oceanic Harmony's Embrace

The jellyfish dance with glee,
While crabs boogie like they're free.
Fish gossip in glittered schools,
Saying humans just are fools.

Seagulls squawk with such delight,
They steal your fries in broad daylight.
Octopuses juggle seashells wide,
And dolphins surf the ocean tide.

Turtles wearing shades so cool,
Follow the latest dolphin school.
Mermaids play cards, a splashy mess,
Everyone's laughing, feeling blessed.

With waves that tickle your toes,
And seaweed that playfully grows.
There's magic in every salty splash,
Come join this bubbly, joyous bash!

Mystical Depths of Blue

The fish wear hats of coral bright,
Throwing a party every night.
Pufferfish puff like balloons,
Singing their silly fishy tunes.

Turtles tell jokes that flop and flail,
While shrimp rehearse a quirky tale.
Waves giggle as they touch the shore,
Tickling toes, they beg for more.

Starfish clap with bright applause,
Cheering on the little flaws.
Sharks in bow ties swim in style,
They're the life of the ocean aisle!

Bubbles rise with laughter's cheer,
As sea creatures dance, oh so dear.
In the watery depths, there's glee,
Who knew the sea could be so free?

Sirens of the Sapphire Shore

Sirens sing with voices sweet,
While barnacles tap their feet.
Waves roll in with a splashy grin,
Salty air makes the day begin.

Crabs in sunglasses strut around,
While clams make pearls without a sound.
Seashells gossip about the tides,
As fish ride scooters for fun rides.

Gulls on stilts do a dance routine,
While sea cucumbers munch on cuisine.
The sunhats worn by playful rays,
Turn beach days into endless plays.

With laughter bubbling from the deep,
The ocean's secrets, no one keeps.
Come dive in for a jolly cheer,
Where silliness is always near!

Beneath the Celestial Waves

Beneath the waves, where giggles bloom,
The sea anemones dance to their tune.
Nautilus twirls like a ballerina,
While fish wear crowns like a big diva.

With sandy castles, crabs stand guard,
Watching clumsy humans working hard.
Eels put on a wig for a show,
Grinning as they put on a glow.

Starfish wink with a cheeky stare,
They slightly flip with style and flair.
The seaweed sways with rhythmic ease,
Hoping to catch a giggling breeze.

In this watery world, playful and bright,
Every splash brings pure delight.
Join the fun where laughter flows,
In the deep blue where the joy just grows!

Embrace of the Ocean's Breath

Beneath a sky so wide and blue,
Seagulls squawk, they steal your stew!
The sunbeam dances on the waves,
While mermaids giggle in their caves.

A crab in a tux, he brews some tea,
Sipping laughter from a salty spree.
The fish wear hats and throw a ball,
While dolphins play, they splash and sprawl.

A fishy joke flops through the air,
'The sea's on a diet, but I don't care!'
As octopi sing, in tune, in time,
With bubbles bursting, a silly rhyme.

So, grab your float and ride the waves,
With clownfish jokes, the ocean braves.
The tides will tickle, the sea will laugh,
In this watery world, all joy we craft.

Symphony of Brine and Bliss

A whale in a hat conducts the show,
With starfish clapping, putting on a glow.
The melodies rise, and the currents sway,
While shrimps do a dance in their own ballet.

A little clam plays the spoons with glee,
While jellyfish waltz so floatily.
The seaweed rustles, like an old deep song,
As fish join the chorus, all night long.

With bubbles popping like festive cheer,
Turtles join in, shifting from gear.
The ocean's orchestra plays loud and proud,
As sea otters laugh, forming a crowd.

So float on your raft and hear the tune,
In this watery world, beneath the moon.
With every splash, let your spirit rise,
In this symphony of fun, under the skies.

Resonance of the Raging Tide

The waves crash in with a joyful shout,
While crabs on the beach play tag about.
Seashells chuckle, as they race the foam,
With every splash, chaos feels like home.

A gull swoops down with a sandwich prize,
The seaglass twinkles, under sunny skies.
While barnacles gossip, stuck on a rock,
Fish throw a party, what a jolly flock!

With flippers flapping, they dip and dive,
In this ocean rhythm, all feels alive.
A shark spins round, "Just a prank, I swear!"
With laughter ringing, joy fills the air.

So ride the tide and let out a cheer,
Surrounded by nonsense, with friends so dear.
In this frothy world, where silliness reigns,
The rhythms of laughter are hard to restrain.

Voyage to the Hidden Abyss

In a vessel made of butter and bread,
We set sail down where the octopus led.
With jellybean sails and a chocolaty mast,
We're bound for the depths, but we're having a blast!

The squids play cards in the twilight's glow,
While anglerfish giggle—what a strange show!
A treasure map scribbled in ketchup and fries,
Adventures await beneath coral skies.

With each silly quest, we trade our wits,
Like finding lost glasses, which none of us fits.
A dolphin proclaims, "Are we almost there?"
"Just past the kraken, it won't be a scare!"

So off we sail, with joy as our guide,
Love's in the air, like the rising tide.
In the hidden abyss, where laughter rings bright,
We cherish the wonders of the deep, delight!

Cradled by the Sea's Arms

In a boat made of jelly, I paddle with glee,
The fish in their tuxedos all laughing at me.
Seagulls play tag with my hat on the run,
While I serenade dolphins, oh what silly fun!

Waves tickle my toes, as I dance on the shore,
And crabs try to join, but they trip and they roar.
Turtles wear sunglasses, they're ready for sun,
And jellyfish giggle; oh, what a great pun!

Shells sing sweet ballads, treasures from the deep,
While starfish applaud with a laugh that could leap.
Mermaids are juggling, they put on a show,
I'm here for the laughter, not just the flow!

So here's to the ocean, that whimsical friend,
With waves full of laughter that never do end.
We'll sail through the silliness, come join in the spree,
For life's a grand joke when you're cradled by sea!

Glistening Memories of Waves

The sun's like a pancake, golden and round,
While sea turtles dive in to flip and to bound.
Splashing and laughing, they wiggle with cheer,
Even fish wear bow ties; they're here for the beer!

Each wave brings a chuckle, a giggle, a sigh,
As crabs clink their claws and wave 'goodbye' high.
Seagulls squawk jokes, they're the stand-up delight,
As I'm rolling in sand, what a whimsical sight!

Shimmering seashells, like whispers of fate,
Tell tales of the fish who believed they were great.
With every small splash, I'm swept in the fun,
A frolicsome dance, oh, we're never done!

When waves shimmer brightly, they tell a true tale,
Of mermaid escapades, and mischief at sail.
So raise up your mugs, let the laughter replay,
In this land of glimmer, where waves go astray!

Where Dreams Meet the Horizon

A ship made of doughnuts sails sweetly along,
With marshmallow clouds, and a gummy bear song.
Skipper's a puppy, with shades on his nose,
He jokes with the jellyfish, everyone knows!

As rainbows of fish jump and splash in the light,
Pirates steal cookies; oh, what a delight!
The horizon is laughing with a cheeky grin,
As I toss in my worries; oh, let the fun begin!

Seashells are giggling, they whisper 'hooray,'
For dreams tangled up in the waves want to play.
With balloons in the air, and a captain's big hat,
We sail through the silliness, imagine that!

So grab all your friends, let's chart a new course,
For laughter and joy are the true driving force.
Where dreams meet the waves, let's dance and let free,
This is our adventure; just wait and you'll see!

Sails Whispering to the Stars

Under a sky filled with glittery beams,
Our sails are a tapestry woven from dreams.
Stars nod in agreement; they chuckle and flare,
As we float on the ocean, a whimsical air!

The wind tells us stories from long, long ago,
Of bananas dressed as pirates who stole the show.
Coconuts are laughing, not one takes offense,
As we dance on the waves, in this silly suspense!

Even the moon joins our raucous delight,
With a winking grin that twinkles so bright.
We're painting the night with our laughter and play,
When sails whisper secrets, we just drift away!

So here's to the stars, our whimsical nest,
With winds that are playful, we're truly blessed.
As sails whisper softly, we sail through the fun,
In this sea of enchantment, where laughter's just begun!

Lullabies of the Deep Blue

Bubbles rise and fish all sing,
A clam turns into a drama king.
Seaweed sways in a jazzy groove,
Crabs do the cha-cha and really move.

Octopus has eight left feet,
With jellyfish doing a happy beat.
Starfish lounging, sipping tea,
Waves crash soft, oh what glee!

Seahorse plays a tiny flute,
While sharks just dance in their sharp-toothed suit.
Whales make jokes that make you laugh,
While dolphins calculate the perfect path.

Underwater vibes are quite the show,
With fish gossiping in a flow.
Deep blue hugs, oh what a scheme,
Dreams drift by like a silly dream.

Serenade of Sirens

Mermaids sing with voices bright,
Enticing sailors in the night.
But wait, they've lost their golden combs,
Now singing with hair brushes in foams.

A ship sailed in with sails so tattered,
Captain danced, the crew just chattered.
Sirens giggle, lure them in,
As fish join in, let the fun begin!

Gulls chirp jokes overhead,
While sea turtles nod and spread.
They laugh so loud, the sea shakes too,
With froggy fish jumping through and through.

Oh, wandering soul, heed the call,
Join the party, don't be small!
In the splash of joy, take a dive,
Where laughter flows and dreams come alive.

Nautical Reveries Unbound

A ship with sails made of hotcakes,
Pirates flip flapjacks, oh what breaks!
Sea oddities play a sweet little tune,
While mermaids dance under a silver moon.

The captain's hat is a fishy charade,
With seagulls squawking, 'What a parade!'
Barnacles tell tales of old,
While squids juggle treasures, daring and bold.

Tropical fruits float in the sea,
Where laughter flows, just like a spree.
Coconut drinks in hand with cheer,
Who says the ocean's nothing to fear?

So dive into this watery realm,
Where every whim is at the helm.
Jellybeans swim, and laughter reigns,
In nautical bliss, forget your chains.

Secrets of the Coral Kingdom

In the coral castle, colors abound,
Fish wear crowns, spinning round!
Anemones giggle, they dance and sway,
As clowns in stripes put on a play.

Bubbles pop like tiny balloons,
Turtles serenade to funny tunes.
Coral beds spark joy in pink,
While hermit crabs wear shoes and wink.

Nemo's cousins throw a ball,
And sea cucumbers stick to the wall.
Everybody's dressed in bright, silly styles,
While laughter echoes through coral aisles.

Secrets flow in waves of fun,
Under the ocean, where life's a run!
So come along, bring your zest,
In this kingdom, you're a welcomed guest.

Echoes of the Endless Deep

Bubbles rise like tiny thoughts,
Fish hold a school, tying knots.
Mermaids giggle, pinching tails,
As sailors search for wind-filled sails.

Octopuses dance with eight left feet,
Claiming treasure, but it's just some sweet.
A crab in a bowtie stamps his feet,
Saying, "It's a ball, come take a seat!"

The seagulls squawk with such delight,
Trading their catch for a raucous flight.
Jellyfish waltz in graceful arcs,
While pirates chase the squeaking larks.

Laughter echoes through the waves,
Where a seaweed band plays tunes that rave.
If laughter's treasure, we're all quite rich,
In this jolly ride, not a single hitch.

Glistening Horizons Unfurled

Seagulls sport shades, such a sight,
Sunbathers compete for the sun's warm light.
A dolphin laughs, flips through the air,
As conch shells whisper, 'Do you dare?'

Flamingos strut with flair, oh my!
Palm trees wave as breezes sigh.
Snorkelers giggle, reeling in rays,
Catching more laughs than fish on their trays.

The sun kicks back, sipping on fun,
While crabs do a dance, not on the run.
Shellfish gossip, sharing the tide,
In this sea of joy, no place to hide!

With footprints drawing tales in the sand,
A beach ball bounces, oh so grand.
Echoes of joy, under the sky,
In the funny shores, time floats by.

Beneath the Celestial Waves

Clowns in the ocean throw a fiesta,
With bubbles and giggles, what a jester!
Anemones wave, wearing big smiles,
While starfish compete in silly styles.

Gummy fish swim in a swirl of jest,
Hiding from shells, they jest and jest.
Turtles in shades, strumming on seashells,
Hum a tune that even the whale tells.

Fishermen pout, "No luck today!"
While mermaids tease with games they play.
Seas parted bright under laughter's grace,
Creating ripples in this funny place.

Floats and flops, a slippery race,
In this deep blue, we've found our space.
Where smiles are cast like nets in the sea,
And every moment's a comedic spree.

Driftwood Poetics

Driftwood stories float by, my friend,
Tales of laughter that never end.
A fish in a top hat shared a joke,
While a beach ball exploded, oh what a poke!

Seashells convene for a gossip chat,
Debating whether they're more 'wit' or 'pat.'
Crabs wear their best suits, ready to dine,
Sipping on seafoam, feeling just fine.

Under the sun, the waves give a chuckle,
Seagulls tweet messages, causing a ruffle.
Sandcastles wave with a melting grin,
As tourists laugh at the tide's goofy spin.

So gather your giggles and cast them wide,
In this realm where humor won't hide.
For every wave brings a fresh, new joke,
In driftwood poetics, having a poke!

Whispers of Aquatic Eden

In a realm where fish wear hats,
And crabs dance like fancy cats,
The jellyfish float with a sway,
Laughing, they brighten the day.

Octopus serves with a grin,
His cocktails finish with a spin,
While seahorses play in a band,
They strum on seaweed, oh so grand!

Turtles race in their slow style,
Pretending they can run a mile,
As dolphins crack a joke or two,
Splashing around, just me and you.

This world beneath is quite bizarre,
With sponge and guppy as our stars,
So swim along, let's not be rude,
We'll giggle in this watery mood.

Waves of Celestial Serenity

Where seagulls wear their Sunday best,
And oysters sing a bluesy jest,
Waves giggle, crashing on the shore,
Sandy toes always wanting more.

The seaweed twirls in joyful dance,
As crabs engage in a silly prance,
Starfish throw a confetti surprise,
In a sea of laughter, oh how time flies!

Mermaids trade their tales and puns,
Shimmering under the golden suns,
While fishy friends play peek-a-boo,
Making waves just for me and you.

With bubbles floating high and free,
The flirting waves call out to thee,
Let's make a splash, don't be a bore,
In this whimsical aquatic shore.

Beneath the Coral Celestials

In realms where shells hold secret glee,
The clownfish giggles, come see me!
Corals paint in colors bright,
Crafting tales in the morning light.

Shrimp hold court with their tiny chairs,
Telling jokes that float through the airs,
A sea horse spins, a dazzling sight,
As starfish laugh under the moonlight.

A wise old turtle gives a wink,
While pondering how much we can drink,
With seaweed shakes and shells of cheer,
Let's toast to worlds we hold so dear!

In this whimsical underwater sprawl,
The laughter echoes, it's our carnival,
With every ripple, come join the fun,
Where humor and tides shall never shun.

Elysium Beneath the Tides

Amidst the depths where bubbles swirl,
A mermaid tosses a twirling pearl,
Fish don their finest, with flair they tread,
While starry-eyed narwhals dance ahead.

Seaglass shimmers, a sparkling view,
While sea cucumbers join in on cue,
They giggle in harmony, bright and loud,
In the underwater carnival crowd.

The octopus juggles the ocean's fate,
As seahorses cheer, it's never too late,
To join the laughter, to share a smile,
In a paradise, a watery mile.

From coral nooks to sandy beds,
Where every fish spins wondrous threads,
Let's relish the joy that the ocean brings,
In this funny world, where laughter sings.

Voyage to the Enchanted Depths

On a ship made of jelly, we sail with delight,
The fish wear their ties, what a curious sight!
Crab cakes are laughing, while seagulls debate,
About who's the fairest, it's quite the great fate.

Octopus serving, he's mixing a brew,
With a cocktail of seaweed and green aquatic too.
The dolphins are dancing, they twirl with a twist,
And I can't help but wonder what else I have missed!

Our captain is sardine, quite proud of his hat,
He sways with the waves, isn't that just a spat?
Shells play the banjo, the sea cucumbers hum,
And we'd join their fun, if we weren't feeling numb.

So let's raise a toast to this wacky brigade,
For nothing's as silly as an ocean parade!
With laughter and bubbles, we sail ever free,
Oh, what a grand voyage, just you wait and see!

Secrets of Tranquil Waters

Beneath the calm waves, a mischief unfolds,
Even fish wear sunglasses, it's all very bold.
The turtles are gossiping, shades of bright green,
While seaweed does the cha-cha, the goofiest scene.

A clam tells a secret about the coral bright,
That it swiped the seashells, a criminal plight.
The seahorses giggle, exchanging fine jokes,
While shrimp throw a party for whimsical folks.

Starfish are painting, with colors so fine,
But they can't find the brushes, oh, what a decline!
With giggles and snickers, we float on the tide,
In seas of pure laughter, where whimsy won't hide.

So come take a dip in our watery bliss,
Where the ocean is silly, you wouldn't want to miss!
We'll uncork the bubbles, let giggles arise,
In this realm of the wacky, beneath sunny skies!

Echoes of the Endless Deep

In the ocean so vast, where the silliness glows,
There's a fish with a toupee, and he strikes quite a pose!
Whales sing in harmony, but please don't dismay,
It's just their way of laughing, hey, what can I say?

Crabs juggle sea urchins, it's pure acrobat flair,
While plankton play hopscotch without any care.
The eel pulls a prank, he hides in a shell,
He pops out and yells, "Surprise! Howdy, fellas!"

The mermaids are giggling, with bubbles in tow,
As they flip through their hair, putting on quite a show.
They toss pearls in the air, all shiny and bright,
To show off their treasure, it's stunning delight!

So join in the fun of this underwater spree,
Where laughter is plenty and everyone's free.
With echoes of joy bouncing all through the deep,
In this world of enchantment, it's the best kind of leap!

A Symphony in Salt and Sea

In a quirky crescendo, the waves clap their hands,
As crabs play maracas, oh, isn't it grand?
The fish join the chorus, with fins in the air,
They whistle and chuckle, as they dance without care.

A seaweed conductor waves his green baton,
While dolphins do pirouettes, from dusk until dawn.
With a splash and a twirl, they take center stage,
In this oceanic ballet, where buoyancy's the rage!

Clams keep the rhythm, with a steady, soft clap,
While jellyfish float in, adorned with great flair,
The starfish are clapping, their five arms in sync,
While the whole ocean giggles, and gives us a wink!

So lend us an ear as we dance on the sea,
In this symphony salty, where everyone's free!
With laughter and music, we'll sail and we'll cheer,
For in this realm of fun, there's naught to fear!

Guardians of the Tidal Realm

At the ocean's door, where sea crabs dance,
Mermaids play poker, taking a chance.
A whale in a tux, with a monocle,
Bids 'fins up!' as it swims, feeling full.

Octopuses juggle with jellyfish bright,
While seahorses race in a comical fight.
The dolphins all giggle, making a fuss,
Telling fish tales while aboard a bus.

A sea turtle scolds a crab for his mess,
Saying, "This beach is not just for excess!"
A clam jumps up, with a wink and a grin,
"No pearls for you until you let me in!"

In the tides we play, in laughter we bask,
In this tidal realm, we find joy in the task.

Reflections in the Crystal Deep

In waters clear, where the fish all preen,
A pufferfish tries on a crown like a queen.
Starfish critique, with their armchair flair,
"Who knew that seashells needed such care?"

A crab in sunglasses, oh what a sight,
Chasing its shadow, day turns to night.
A fish stocks its pantry with sushi galore,
Only to find it's just seaweed more.

Sea cucumbers gossip, so terribly slow,
While coral reefs giggle at the fashion show.
Clownfish wear ties, in hues so bizarre,
Dear jellyfish float around, no avatar.

Laughing reflections in the shimmering light,
Echoing joy as day fades to night.

Labyrinth of Waves and Wonders

In twisty turns where the seaweed sways,
Fish keep their secrets through complex ways.
Jellyfish float like balloons in the sun,
Inviting all to join in on the fun.

A dolphin decides to host a grand spree,
While anchovies practice their synchronized glee.
Crabs break out dance moves, so jazzy and neat,
While a sea star keeps the rhythm and beat.

In caverns deep, where shadows do creep,
Anemones giggle, their secrets to keep.
"Who's the fairest?" they whisper and tease,
While clams hold their shells in mock-royal ease.

Waves roll and tumble, laughter unfurls,
In this underwater maze, joy swirls.

Journey to Aquatic Dreams

On a ship made of seafoam, we venture wide,
With an octopus captain, bursting with pride.
A seagull in shades, makes a snarky remark,
As they sail through the sunset, igniting a spark.

Fish wearing hats form a parade on the sand,
While seahorses dance with their tails hand-in-hand.
Crabcakes do cartwheels, peeking for cheer,
While the mermaids giggle and toast with cold beer.

The waves sing their songs with a bubbly refrain,
As dolphins conspire to do it again.
A walrus in flip-flops strolls without care,
In this aquatic dreamland, all laughter we share.

Together we frolic, our spirits will soar,
In this ocean of joy, we always want more!

Odyssey of the Siren's Call

A mermaid sings with a voice so sweet,
Telling fish tales and tales of feet.
A sailor slips on a banana peel,
Now he's dancing with seals, what a surreal feel!

The dolphins giggle, they swim in glee,
While capricious crabs throw a party with tea.
The waves are chuckling, making quite a fuss,
As the captain shouts, 'Stop the hullabaloo, thus!'

The seaweed waltzes, it's quite the sight,
Each bubble popping gives us a fright.
With tides that tickle and currents that tease,
We sail with laughter, riding the breeze!

Beneath the Glittering Blue

Beneath the surface, life's a blast,
Where fish wear shades and swim by fast.
A turtle twirls in a party hat,
While octopuses juggle, can you believe that?

The coral reefs laugh, their colors bright,
As fish with funny fins dart left and right.
A whale cracks jokes, causing quite a wave,
While a shy seahorse tries to behave.

Mermen and mermaids, all in a line,
Compete in slurring up seaweed wine.
Dancing through bubbles, no worries in sight,
Life under the waves is simply delight!

Whirlpools of Memory

Whirlpools spin tales of days gone by,
With squids and seals, who always supply.
An anchor gets tangled in seaweed's embrace,
While sailors onboard just grin in their place.

With a wink and a splash, the clownfish parade,
Juggling sea urchins, oh what a charade!
They swirl and they twirl, making us laugh,
At memories swimming in this oceanic path.

Crashing waves chuckle at moments we share,
As barnacles tell the wildest affair.
Frogs in a lighthouse sing tunes so bright,
Every day is a treasure, pure ocean delight!

Eternal Embrace of the Water

In a splash of fun, we wade on through,
With jellyfish jokes, oh who knew?
A sea turtle claims he's the race champ,
But I think he just likes the shade in the damp.

Fish flip and flop, doing sea dance moves,
While crustaceans throw down, they groove in their grooves.
A pelican drops by, cracks a fresh pun,
And the waves roll on, oh what fun has begun!

As the foam tickles toes and lessons unfold,
Even sea stars shine with stories untold.
With salt on our lips and laughter so light,
We'll float in this joy, a pure ocean night!

Shores of Dreams and Distant Stars

On sandy shores where seagulls squawk,
Mermaids munch on seaweed salad,
A crab in shades does a funny walk,
While jellyfish dance, oh so pallid.

The starfish gossip, quite the chat,
About the octopus with too much flair,
They giggle at the old, tired brat,
Who can't seem to style his tangled hair.

Waves roll in with a bubbling sound,
They tickle toes and tease the shore,
While playful dolphins spin around,
And steal the beach ball—oh, what a chore!

The sun sets low, paints skies in pink,
As crabs toast marshmallows with glee,
In this grand tale, let's stop and think,
Life's a splash, oh, what a spree!

Allure of the Celestial Sea

Up above, the stars grow bright,
While fish wear goggles, oh what a sight,
Dolphins laugh at the kite in flight,
Making jokes of the moon's soft light.

An octopus claims he's a fashion star,
In a shell he wears that's quite bizarre,
But the turtle hums from near afar,
Saying styles change, just look at your car!

The waves bring tales of mermaid pranks,
One zapped a sailor with a fishy wink,
They giggle and swim, banking their tanks,
While sea cucumbers dance, what do you think?

As the tides rise high, a splash is made,
A water fight breaks, with laughter and cheer,
With every wave, good vibes cascade,
In this ocean of fun, let's cuddle near!

A Haven in the Swell

In the swell where the sun shines bright,
Fish wear hats, and crabs party at night,
With clams and oysters jiving with delight,
Every wave a tune, a cheery sight.

A whale with a wink pulls a funny prank,
Squirting water on a dolphin's flank,
The coral orchestra plays, no need to tank,
As starfish giggle, their sides they flank.

On surfboards made of driftwood and cheer,
Seagulls glide and glister with glee,
Every splash a giggle, every cheer a tear,
In this twilight party, oh let it be!

When the sun dips low, a dance starts to churn,
The waves do a twirl, the seafoam will yearn,
In this haven, we laugh, and we learn,
The sea's full of joy, and life's just a turn!

Secrets Beneath Wave's Crest

Under the crests where secrets lie,
A crab starts telling tales with a sigh,
Of fish that wore ties and danced in the sky,
While cucumbers grooved, oh me, oh my!

A narwhal sings of a restaurant's zest,
With soup made of seaweed, known as the best,
A clam clarified the menu with jest,
As everyone waited, eager and dressed.

Octopuses play cards, four hands in tow,
While turtles slow dance, moving too slow,
The seashells cheer, "Look at that show!"
Beneath the waves, the fun seems to flow.

As the tides change course, stories are spun,
Of octopuses dreaming of having more fun,
In this aquatic world, we're never quite done,
Life's a grand ship, and we all are the sun!

Celestial Dancers of the Blue

Fish in tuxedos glide and twirl,
As jellyfish float in a glittering whirl.
Starfish hold hands, oh what a sight,
Under the moon, they party all night.

Coral reefs hum a silly tune,
While seahorses waltz beneath the moon.
The crabs do the cha-cha with style,
As dolphins jump in a bubbly pile.

A whale brings the snacks, a great big feast,
An octopus plays the drums, quite the beast!
A shrimp steals the show with a little dance,
Laughs echoed underwater, oh what a chance!

So if you seek laughter, join this spree,
In the depths of the blue, where the fun is free.
Dancing with creatures, oh what a dream,
In the ocean's grand party, all together we beam.

Shores of Eternal Wonder

Sandy castles built high with flair,
Seagulls squawking without a care.
The crabs hold a race, oh what a sight,
With flags made of shells, they dash with delight.

Shell hunters gather, with hopes to find
The biggest of treasures, both rare and unkind.
A sand dollar whispers a secret or two,
While starfish giggle, 'We're not all that blue!'

The tides bring tales of sea monsters long,
While mermaids sing with their favorite song.
A wise old turtle shouts, 'Hurry up, friends!
Let's feast on the seaweed before it all ends!'

And when the sun sets, painting skies gold,
The laughter of waves in stories retold.
For on these shores, with each grain of sand,
Lies endless amusement, hand in fin, hand.

Tidal Serenades

Waves do the limbo, low and high,
While fish flash by, whoosh! Oh my!
The tide sings songs of joy and glee,
With crabs snapping their claws, 'Come dance with me!'

Seashell horns blow a comical tune,
As the ocean frolics under the moon.
A dolphin's flips create quite the splash,
While a goofy octopus makes quite the rash.

With every ripple, a giggle escapes,
Maritime fun with curious shapes.
The seagulls play tag, diving and swooping,
While sea urchins hide, their faces drooping.

So join in the laughter, let the waves play,
With silliness soaring throughout the day.
In every tide's embrace, joy is our friend,
Where tides are the serenades that never end.

Oceans of Lullabies

Cradled by currents, the seaweed sways,
As bubbles burst forth in playful displays.
A narwhal hums tunes, sweet as can be,
While clownfish chuckle in harmony.

A sleepy old turtle, slow and wise,
Winks at the waves with twinkling eyes.
Pufferfish puff, a sight to behold,
As eels crack jokes while the tales are retold.

With lullabies whispered by each gentle wave,
Embraces of currents, so tender and brave.
A starfish dreams big, wishing on a star,
While sea cucumbers munch in their jar.

In these watery depths, a giggle rings clear,
Through oceans of laughter, there's nothing to fear.
So float with the tides, let your heart come alive,
In lullabies sung, we're all sure to thrive.

Cradle of the Ocean's Heart

A dolphin danced in a fancy hat,
He asked a crab to join in and chat.
The waves giggled as they splashed about,
While a seagull tried to steal a sprout.

The fish were playing leapfrog with grace,
But a whale sneezed and changed the place.
The seaweed waved, oh what a sight,
As jellyfish twirled with pure delight.

A treasure chest sang a silly tune,
While octopuses played cards in the moon.
A clam told a joke that made all shells crack,
And crabs wore tuxedos, brought laughter back!

Bubbles floated like balloons of cheer,
Underwater giggles covered the sphere.
In this grand jest of the ocean's art,
Every fin and fin fun—oh, what a start!

The Voyage of Stars Beneath

A ship with sails made of cotton candy,
Set sail with a pig dressed quite dandy.
The captain, a turtle with glasses on tight,
Steered through the sea, oh what a sight!

A group of fish held a disco ball,
With seaweed streamers decorating the hall.
The starfish brokedance under moonlight,
While crabs clinked cocktails, all feeling quite right.

As clouds gathered round for a great snack,
The peanuts fell in—there's none to lack!
A seahorse shimmied, it's quite the affair,
While mermaids giggled, with jewels to share.

The waves hummed tunes of the deep blue sea,
Fluttering finned friends, so wild and free.
In this journey, oh what a dance,
With laughter and joy, they all took a chance!

Luminous Skies Over Wavy Horizons

Under a sky like a rainbow's end,
The lobsters planned a party to send.
With popcorn and jellybeans in a heap,
The sea creatures laughed, forgetting to sleep.

The pufferfish bounced on a trampoline,
While clownfish juggled, all in between.
They donned their shades, acting so cool,
As crabs played chess with an octopus's rule.

A stingray skated, what a fine show!
While turtles skateboarded, putting on flow.
The whirlpool laughed, and the whirlpool swirled,
Creating a merry-go-round, oh what a world!

With fireworks bursting like shells in the night,
The ocean's delight danced to the right.
Every splash held a giggle or cheer,
In this wavy paradise, everyone dear!

Chronicles of the Tidal Realm

In the tides where the jellybeans grow,
A kraken tried knitting with strings in a row.
He tangled his tentacles, oh what a sight,
While fish whirled around in sheer delight.

A clam wrote a story, to everyone's glee,
About a fish who dreamed of flying free.
With pages of bubbles, he turned them with grace,
As seagulls kept laughing, flying all over the place.

The tides conspired to steal a fish fry,
But the fish threw confetti and began to fly.
A little eel sang, shaking with laughter,
As the calypso waves played music thereafter.

Each splash brought a tale, a giggle, a cheer,
With wise old turtles who'd lend you an ear.
In this rollicking tide, where laughter is found,
Every wave shares a joy that knows no bound!

Serenade of Coral Castles

Bubbles sing in sunny rays,
Fish in bow ties dance and sway.
Jellybeans float on currents bright,
Mermaids joke with sheer delight.

Seahorses wear their finest suits,
Clams play cards in seaweed boots.
Giggling waves tease sandy shores,
Crabs in tuxedos, such fine chores!

Octopus joins with juggling flair,
Whales are laughing in mid-air.
Fins and tails in harmony,
A deep-sea show for you and me.

In this realm of glee so vast,
Ocean's humor unsurpassed.
Join the dance, take off your shoes,
In these waters, you can't lose!

Journey through Liquid Light

Sailing where the sunbeams play,
Squids are painting in a ray.
Flippers flip and bubbles pop,
In this world, the fun won't stop.

With a wink, the dolphins glide,
Stars align in ocean's tide.
Crabs enact a comedy,
Tickling fish, oh what a spree!

Turtles tell the silliest jokes,
Blowing bubbles, laughing folks.
Clownfish burst forth in a jest,
This deep-sea trip is truly blessed!

As we glide through water's hue,
Join the antics, laugh anew.
Adventure calls, don't be shy,
In this ocean, we can fly!

Adrift in a Crystal Mirror

Floating on a shimmering tide,
A starfish spins, a joyful ride.
Mirrors glint with fish that tease,
While seaweed sways like a gentle breeze.

Giant clams throw a costume ball,
Seashells sparkle and enthrall.
Nautical nonsense fills the scene,
With winks of winkles, oh so keen!

Glowfish glow with colors bright,
Flirting under the moonlight.
Upside down, the ocean laughs,
With jellyfish, they share their gaffs.

In this twilight, we won't frown,
Everything's fun, never down.
With each splash, echoes of cheer,
Let's celebrate, the time is here!

Tales from the Depths of Bliss

Swirling tales of joy unfold,
Eels wear scarves of blue and gold.
Giggling gulls share stories wild,
Every wave, with laughter, piled.

Anemones wave like they're alive,
In this snug and wavy hive.
Silly squids with their inkwell pens,
Write comedies that never ends.

Crabby chefs stir up the stew,
While fishes chant a tune or two.
The sea's a stage for all to play,
In every splash, a new bouquet.

So come and dive into the fun,
Dance with rays, or just outrun.
In this deep, we're all aglow,
Bringing laughter, don't you know?

www.ingramcontent.com/pod-product-compliance
Lightning Source LLC
Chambersburg PA
CBHW072218070526
44585CB00015B/1389